Retirement Sucks

A Guide for Men

FRITZ FUHS

ISBN-13: 978-1505907223
ISBN-10: 1505907225

DEDICATION

To my very special wife.

CONTENTS

ACKNOWLEDGMENTS

The help and feedback from my family has been greatly appreciated.

i

INTRODUCTION

It took me over twenty years to write this book because it took me over twenty years to adjust to retirement. I have placed after each chapter title the month and year in which I wrote the chapter. This makes it clear to the reader that my adjustment to retirement was a gradual transition, involving the development of a new lifestyle. I believe my book can help retiring men make the adjustment in a shorter period of time with less frustration.

1
QUESTIONS
JANUARY, 1992

It seemed sensible to retire. I still loved the job and was probably more effective than ever, at least through Wednesday, but I became so tired by the middle of each week that Thursday and Friday were no longer enjoyable. Our last child had left the nest. My wife (seven years younger than I) had reentered the work force after thirty years of being a very effective homemaker, and enjoyed her job, but she didn't like coming home to the household chores after a day on the job. My employer had an early retirement bonus that was substantial enough to make my retirement at sixty-two financially feasible. So, I retired. Now, eight months later, I have some questions. I don't have any answers yet, but I do have questions about how a man (these problems are not necessarily the same for a woman) is supposed to adjust to retirement in our present society.

First question: What am I, now that I have retired? On any form that I fill out, where it asks "employment?", I used to put the word, "counselor". Now I put the word, "Retired", which doesn't tell anyone what I do. It just implies that I do nothing. The first question that most people ask you when they discover that you have retired is, "What are you doing now that you're retired?" I am still fulfilling the roles of husband, father, and grandfather such as I did before retirement (actually much better), but that doesn't seem to be a very satisfactory answer. At this point I'm not sure what I am. I think that I'm experiencing an identity crises.

Second question: As a retired person, am I still productive? This

1

question first occurred to me at a family gathering when my brother-in-law (in his 50's and very productive) stated that he was beginning to believe that euthanasia might serve a definite need, since there was truly no point in society supporting a person after they were no longer productive. I asked what he meant by "productive". He said that was when you could still hold a regular job that produced something for society. It didn't bother me that I was no longer productive according to his definition. It did concern me that he was also (unintentionally I'm sure) including his beautiful eighty-two year old mother who is the glue that holds this extended family together. Even though traveling requires an enormous effort on her part, she appears willingly at grandchildren's weddings, great grandchildren's baptisms, and even new housewarmings halfway across the country.

Third question: Am I worth less now that I have retired? I am no longer sure what it is that determines a person's value. As a counselor, I used to tell junior high students (many had a feeling of no self worth) that each of us were of infinite value based solely on the fact that we were human beings. But the fact remains that I feel much less important now that I am retired. Why should retirement affect my feeling of self worth? One of the reasons is the look in other people's eyes when you tell them you are retired. There might be a fleeting moment of envy, but it is quickly replaced by a look of condescending pity. My wife says that this is all just my imagination, but that doesn't make me feel of any more value. Am I worth less? I tell myself no, but the feeling is still there.

I have been told that many men die shortly after they retire (not as true of women). I think that I am beginning to understand why. If a man can't arrive at satisfactory answers to the three questions that I have asked, his will to live could be greatly diminished. Maybe my quest for the answers will keep me busy in the days to come.

2
ANSWERS
JANUARY, 1995

Question number one: What am I? I have almost accepted the fact that I am no longer a counselor. I might still possess the skills of a counselor, but being a counselor is no longer part of my lifestyle. When a person asks what you are, they actually want to know what you do. In other words, "What is the work you are doing that justifies your existence?"

But I am supposed to be retired. That implies that I am no longer working. Therein lays the problem. A man cannot really live without work. We need a more accurate term to designate this period of time in a man's life after he leaves the routine of the full-time job.

I work as hard now as I have ever worked. But I work at many things. I am able to do this because I no longer have to evaluate each job by the dollar criteria; that is, will it bring in enough money to support the needs of my family? I work at gardening, cooking, writing, exercising, teaching, cleaning, manufacturing, carpentry, and selling, all for my own satisfaction. In addition, I work at volunteering some of my time for the benefit of others.

So, what am I? My happiness is not the result of no longer having to work. Therefore, the new word, which we need to replace the word, "retirement", must imply better, more satisfying work, rather than the end of work. The word must describe a promotion to a state of self employment at one's own discretion. Instead of a retirement, this experience in a man's life involves an arising. Rather than feeling like I have retired, I actually feel as I've been reborn.

Question number two: Am I still productive? I'm still not sure what if means to be productive. When working on a job it is always quite obvious that some workers are more productive than others. Frequently they get paid more money for being more productive. They make more pieces, paint larger areas, cook better food, or design better buildings, and they are rewarded accordingly for their productivity. However, am I being productive when there is no reward other than my own satisfaction?

When I grow flowers in my garden, when I walk the elderly neighbor's dog, when I volunteer to listen to a slow reader read at a local school, when I pick up litter on the neighborhood sidewalk, or when I ride my bike to strengthen my heart, am I being productive? Society obviously profits from such activity even though it doesn't choose to reward it monetarily.

Therefore, for my own peace of mind, I have decided to define productive activity as any activity that positively affects any person's quality of life. That would include one's own quality of life as well as that of another.

Question number three: Am I worth less now that I have retired? Now that I have decided that retirement is not the end of working, but instead the freedom to work at anything one chooses, and now that I have redefined productivity as any activity that positively affects any person's quality of life, I no longer have a feeling of little self worth. A feeling of self worth is dependent on being able to attain a feeling of accomplishment. I have discovered that one need not move a mountain in order to experience such a feeling. One needs only to reach a desired goal, no matter how insignificant it may seem to others. The first step, of course, is to set a goal. Then a man must organize his time sufficiently to make achieving the goal possible. This is an area in which many retired men have a problem.

3
MANAGING
FEBRUARY 1995

Organizing the use of one's time is a skill. Many retired men have had no reason to learn this skill. Their boss told them how to use their time on the job, and their family's needs determined how they would use their time at home. Women, however, especially in the role of homemaker, must make numerous daily decisions on how they are going to use their time.

When a man retires, he is immediately confronted with the need to plan the use of large blocks of time on a daily basis. Having had little or no experience in time management, the new experience of trying to decide what to do with himself can prove to be frighteningly frustrating.

I discovered early in retirement that I had to develop some kind of a method to even succeed in remembering to do the things that I wanted to do. A folded three by five card and a pen carried in my pocket at all times have helped considerably. With these available tools I am able to write down anything I encounter that I want to remember to do. When it's accomplished, I cross it out. Each Sunday, after church, I make out a new card for the coming week. Checking my card at breakfast each morning has become a part of my daily routine.

One side of my card has also become a place to write down anything that I want to remember. It might be a new telephone number, the name of a new acquaintance, or the name of a video or book recommended by a friend.

The happiness of any person depends a great deal on how they spend their free time. Since a retired person, by definition, has more free time than committed time, how he spends it is of the utmost importance.

Occasionally, one encounters a retired person who insists that he is busier than he had ever been with practically no free time at all. Upon examining such a person's daily routine, you frequently find that he is still allowing other people to decide how he spends his time. He might be babysitting for his grandchildren, running errands for his wife, or caring for his invalid parents; all commendable activities. However he is learning nothing about managing his time from such activities if he feels that he has no choice in whether or not to do them.

There needs to be a transition period between the lifestyle which consists of the daily routine of a typical job, and the new lifestyle of managing the major part of one's own time.

First of all, when you retire, take the time to methodically clean out the dusty corners of your life. Maybe it's a drawer of pictures that you have never identified. Maybe it's a garden of perennials that you have never divided. Maybe it's a sibling to whom you haven't written a letter in twenty years. Maybe it's a closet full of clothes that even the Salvation Army wouldn't accept. Maybe it's a TV viewing habit that consumes hours of each day from which you profit nothing. Maybe it's a diet that is robbing you of years of healthy living. Maybe it's a "friend" who drains you emotionally on a regular basis.

You can't start a new life carrying all that old baggage, and retirement is a new life. A new life means a new lifestyle. You can't develop a new lifestyle until you critically examine the old one. You now have the time to do so in detail. Tackle one thing at a time and examine it carefully. Examine each aspect of your life according to whether or not it helps you reach your present goals.

4
HEALTH
MARCH 1995

One needs well-defined goals as much at sixty as one needed goals at twenty. Without goals man just exists; with goals he lives. How well he lives will depend on how well he has defined his goals. A basic goal for the older person must be good health. Without it, little else is possible.

With modern medicine and a great deal of effort, anyone can maintain their health sufficiently to accomplish almost anything within their reach. As one ages, it just takes more effort and self discipline.

Diet is a good example. Many nutritious, inexpensive foods are available for the typical, retired person who is willing to expend the extra effort needed to shop wisely and to cook on a regular basis. Even more is available for the person willing to expend the extra effort needed to plan and raise a garden. But even if a person neither cooks nor gardens, they can learn to make intelligent choices. Start by keeping track of everything you eat for a week. Most foods are marked as to nutritional content. If one keeps track of the quantity eaten and the nutritional content of what they have eaten, it is rather easy to arrive at a comparison between what you are consuming and what is recommended for a healthy diet. When I did this, I discovered that the salt and fat content of my diet was more than desirable. There were other things that I had been missing due to a lack of variety in what I was used to eating. Changing my eating habits did not prove to be that difficult.

It's also important to observe closely how our particular body reacts to certain foods. I found that my body for some reason could not tolerate caffeine. I also discovered that I felt much better in the morning if I didn't eat anything during a three or four hour period before I went to bed. When I overeat, I become very tired. These are facts that I have discovered are true concerning my body. They may not be true of anyone else's body on earth.

A mistake made by many persons is a reliance on the medical community to keep them healthy. It is not that doctors are not interested in prevention; it is just that that is not their area of expertise. You are the only person with the power to maintain your health. You are the only one who really knows how you feel under any given circumstance. If you educate yourself to understand what your feelings indicate concerning your health, then you will be in a unique position to keep yourself healthy. However, a person must work at it.

The area of exercise is where the older person must expend the most effort, both physically and emotionally. It is generally agreed among therapists (who know a great deal more about this subject than doctors) that regular exercise is a must for good health. The kind and amount of exercise is where you must be the judge. I believe that my heart attack at fifty-nine was due to the fact that I had never exercised my heart. Being a slow-motion person by nature, even when I did indulge in physical exercise, my heart rate never came close to what is recommended by therapists. However, at fifty-nine I had no desire to run. The typical aerobic exercise didn't appeal to me either. I did find that I could ride a stationary bicycle two or three times a week without giving up due to boredom or fatigue.

It is essential for a person's health that they find, as a member of our largely sedentary society, an exercise that appeals to them sufficiently that they will stick to it on a regular basis. Again, it is a personal decision that you are in a better position to make than anyone else. First, educate yourself concerning your body's need for exercise. Then, on the basis of what you know about your body and how it feels in different situations, choose an exercise that can become a regular part of your lifestyle.

Many older persons suffer from lack of sufficient sleep. Sleep experts agree that this problem is not caused by aging. They recommend the following:

1. Exercise twenty to thirty minutes at least three days a week, but not too close to bedtime.
2. Limit naps to not longer than thirty minutes.
3. Take walks so that you will be exposed to adequate natural daylight.
4. Sleep in a cool, quiet, dark room on a comfortable, supportable mattress.
5. Ask your physician if you're taking medication that may cause daytime drowsiness or nighttime sleeplessness.
6. Don't worry about falling asleep.
7. Avoid caffeine in the evening.
8. Go to bed at the same time each night, and wake up at the same time each morning.
9. Limit drinking liquids a few hours before bedtime, especially alcohol.
10. Don't go to bed too full or too hungry.
11. Develop a ritual by doing the same things each night before going to bed.

I have discovered one more thing about my overall health that means something to me even though I'm not at all sure that I understand it. I spent a lifetime figuring out ways in my daily routine to avoid or lessen the amount of time I spent doing physically hard work. Now that I am retired one would assume that I could avoid all hard work if I so choose. However, I have waited all these years so that I could become deeply immersed in gardening; growing a wide variety of plants just for the sheer pleasure of seeing them grow. Moreover, I have discovered that gardening cannot be accomplished with any degree of true success without a great deal of hard, physical work.

Consequently, I am working harder physically that I have ever worked before. What I have discovered is that the harder I work the better I feel. I no longer worry about getting enough physical exercise to remain healthy. My greatest concern is whether or not I will have the physical stamina to reach the goals I daily set for myself.

5
WORK
JANUARY 1996

Ever since I decided that successful retirement must include work, I have been experimenting with different kinds of work to see if I could arrive at an ideal work for me. It would be work that I enjoyed and also an activity from which I could derive a feeling of accomplishment.

One of the first things I did was organize a group of fellow retirees for the purpose of picking up litter in our respective neighborhoods. We are called the Area Maintenance Person (AMP) organization. We have a specially designed T-Shirt, a very effective litter pick-up device called a Park Patrol, and we meet for a luncheon once a month. Upon joining the AMPs, a retired volunteer is given the T-shirt and the Park Patrol from a fund supported by sponsoring businesses of the community. I do get a genuine feeling of accomplishment from helping keep our community free of litter. Being part of the group has also helped me overcome the feeling of social isolation that comes with retirement for many men.

I have also become involved in other volunteer activities. I serve on the board of a group called Friends of VanderVeer, whose purpose is to support a local botanical garden. I have also helped tutor persons learning English as a second language. Our church maintenance committee has also taken some of my time. These have all been volunteer activities. In all of them, women have been present in much greater numbers than men, and seem to derive a greater sense of accomplishment from volunteering than men do. This might possibly be because men, to a much greater extent than women, have spent most of their lives being evaluated by how much money they have been able to command for their services.

As for paid employment, I tried substitute teaching shortly after I retired. However, I found it too emotionally and physically exhausting, and I decided that I could not do such a commitment justice. I have also taught origami and a method for solving the Rubik's Cube in gifted and talented summer school classes that only meet for three one-hour sessions each day, five days a week, for a two-week period. These I have definitely enjoyed a great deal, and I will continue to teach them as long as the need for them and my good health continue.

This past August, I also agreed to teach a class in Landscape and Horticulture for special needs high school students, for two hours a day, five days a week, for eighteen weeks. I enjoyed teaching the class because I have become intensely interested in gardening since I have retired. It was also educational in an area I love. However, I did not like being committed to a daily obligation and the consequential loss of freedom.

So what have I learned about working during retirement? Although I will continue to do many volunteer jobs because I enjoy them, I now realize that I find a job more emotionally rewarding if I am paid something for my time and effort. This is probably because one can always use extra money no matter how much one has as a regular retirement income.

I have also learned that the freedom to use my time impulsively as I wish is one of the things about retirement that I prize. This freedom is necessary in Iowa even if you are going to get the most out of something as basic as the day-to-day weather. It's also necessary if you are going to get the most out of your personal contacts with your family and friends. It might be a birthday party. It might be a grandchild playing her first volleyball game. It might be a wedding or it might be a funeral.

Many persons fear uncommitted time because of possible boredom. I do think that a retired person is happier if they establish a daily routine. However, for my happiness, this must be a routine that can be interrupted any time something more interesting comes along.

6
PAIN
APRIL 1996

Recently, there has been a great deal in the news about abortion, assisted suicide, alcoholism, drug misuse, and various kinds of mental illness. These are not all directly related to retirement or aging in general, but they do all seem to be related to our present society's obsession with avoiding all pain and suffering. There is something particularly pathetic about the money and effort we seem willing to expend to avoid any kind of physical discomfort.

I think this attitude is particularly relevant to any person wishing to age gracefully. Anytime we experience pain, our body is sending us a message. It is not only unwise to ignore the message, it is even worse to paralyze the messenger. We are being given the impression by drug manufacturers and doctors alike that for every discomfort there is a pill. Even if this were true it would prove to be only a temporary solution to our problem.

Whenever we feel pain, the wise response is to search for the cause. If the cause is a life-threatening problem, then taking a pill to kill the pain could keep us from discovering a disease at a treatable stage. If we find that the cause is not life-threatening, we will then find the pain psychologically easier to handle. I truly believe that aging gracefully involves learning to handle pain without the help of mind-numbing drugs. Much of the therapy recommended for recovering from age-related physical problems involves considerable pain. However, those who have persevered through such therapy will assure you that it was worth it.

It certainly makes sense, in a situation where the cause is known, to take medicine to relieve intense pain. My concern is for the person who expects medicine to take them through the aging process with no pain at all.

I don't believe in pain for pain's sake. There was a time when people inflicted pain upon themselves purposely in order to make them supposedly stronger spiritually. This seems as pointless to me as spending a great deal of our resources avoiding pain. An ordinary day in a person's life can present a sufficient number of unpleasant physical experiences to test one's character. The way we handle these experiences tells a lot about us.

Complaining about an unpleasant experience is rarely appropriate or helpful. Such an experience might very well be of fleeting duration and not reoccur. To quietly endure it not only strengthens our character but places such pain in proper perspective as not a very important occurrence in the day's overall experiences.

The side effects of our avoiding discomfort can also have a negative impact. Riding instead of walking, or using an elevator instead of the stairs robs us of the exercise that will keep us physically healthy.

If there were no pain in a person's life, then pleasure would have less meaning. It would appear that we should expect both, and balance one against the other.

7
SAVORING
MAY, 1997

Entertainment is a word that we all take for granted. Of course we all have things that we enjoy doing. Or do we? Why do so many men after retirement find it difficult to find something to amuse them? It would appear that, for many men, their main source of entertainment before retirement was their work. When they weren't working they were resting. Even on vacation, if they did something for the sheer pleasure of it, they rarely had sufficient time to really enjoy it. Lack of time was probably the culprit. Whatever the cause, I believe that few men in our society ever learn the meaning of the word, savor.

To savor a given experience is to examine it mentally while enjoying it physically. It is also important to do so leisurely and in great detail. Rushing through an experience robs us of the chance to savor. Not rushing seems to be for many persons to be a waste of time, and therefore they never stop to smell the roses.

Once we have retired, we have the time to savor every minute of every day. Don't jump out of bed in the morning. Stretch, and think about how good it feels. A leisurely morning shower wakes me up, and tends to soothe my aching joints. I cook my breakfast, not because I am convinced that hot oatmeal is good for me, but because I really like it, and now I have the time to savor it. Reading the newspaper has also become part of my early morning ritual. I now have the time to keep informed of what is happening in my community. I also have time to savor the humor of the comic strips. Even washing the dishes (I have never been able to savor a dishwasher) on a cold winter morning is something that feels real good.

While I am deciding what I intend to accomplish during the remainder of the morning, weather permitting, I will take a walk through my garden. I have discovered that a garden is never the same two days in a row. It's amazing what can happen overnight. Furthermore, if you happen to like plants, savoring a garden on an early summer morning has to be one of man's most enjoyable experiences. The details are absolutely infinite, if you take the time to examine them.

Savoring is closely related to being aware of detail. In our fast-paced modern society, we seem to be encouraged to forget the detail in order to arrive as quickly as possible at a specific goal. We seem to forget that life is a journey, and if the journey is not truly savored, then we have not really lived.

I have friends who are continually using all of their time and energy to reach a specific goal. When they reach it, they look immediately for another goal. I have other friends who are much more interested in the journey. They reach so few goals that they appear irresponsible. Actually, they are so intrigued by the journey that they become distracted. This leads to their taking a long time to reach a goal, or they actually go off on a tangent, and forget what their original goal was.

I am more convinced every day, especially when one is retired, that savoring the journey is much more important than reaching any goal.

8
GENDER
OCTOBER, 1996

Retiring is a great deal like entering the military service. In the military, you are immediately stripped of your identity and placed in a highly structured program that helps you develop a new and positive self concept. When you retire, you are also stripped of your identity. However, there is no program to help you develop a new and positive self concept.

Retirement is the great equalizer. Nobody cares after you retire if you were important or highly skilled in your working career. Now that you are retired, you are no longer a mason, or a carpenter, or a teacher, or a salesperson, or a doctor, or a horticulturist, or a lawyer, or anything else. You are still a person, but you are nothing that distinguishes you from all other retirees.

It's a little bit like graduating from high school. You need to find a new way to occupy your time, and you need to establish a new lifestyle around your new use of time. The big difference is that you don't have to take the first job you come to when you retire, because the main reason for getting a job will not be for financial support. For probably the first time in your life you can slowly and methodically look around and ideally find an activity that you enjoy, that gives you a sense of accomplishment, and that is flexible in that you can enjoy free time when you wish. If you are paid for doing it, that's nice but not necessary. A retiree should search diligently for such an activity because his physical and his mental health depend on his finding it.

There was a time when retirement meant a well-deserved physical rest after a lifetime of hard, physical work. Retirement meant doing as little as possible in the short period of time you had before death. This is no longer true. Men must now plan for twenty or thirty years of living after their formal retirement. If they have been wise enough to nurture their health throughout their lifetime then retirement can also mean very active living if they so desire.

Most people have favorite activities they have enjoyed in their rare free moments before retirement. They are naturally looking forward to indulging themselves full-time in such activities. These might include golf, traveling, reading, gambling, etc. However, such recreational activities rarely lend themselves satisfactorily to full-time use. Maybe there is insufficient sense of accomplishment, or maybe overuse of such an activity produces boredom. Whatever the reason, a new lifestyle can rarely be built around a recreational activity.

In looking for things to do to fill his time constructively after retirement, a man may also encounter a gender problem. As a man faces declining energy and stamina, he might be attracted to activities that in his culture have traditionally been reserved for women. He might, want to do the cooking, wash the dishes, or clean the house. Even if his wife approves, and many wives will not, these are not the kinds of activities that he can brag about to his male friends.

If he is a gardener and discovers that he and his wife, living alone, have little need for a great deal of vegetable produce, he might start raising flowers. He will eventually discover that men can talk about raising vegetables and possibly roses, but few men will be willing to discuss anything like petunias.

Or possibly he enjoys knitting, or crocheting, or embroidering. It takes a very secure man to do these things and still feel like a man. Men may play golf, fish, hunt, gamble, or play checkers. However, they are not suppose to enjoy shopping, talking on the telephone, or going out for lunch. Everyone involved, both men and women, would be happier if such stereotypical gender roles would gradually dissolve about the time men and women reach their fifties or sixties.

We should all feel free to do anything from which we receive satisfaction and enjoyment as long as we consider it morally acceptable, and it violates no one else's rights or feelings. As women get older they tend to draw emotionally from a group of close female

17

friends. Our society doesn't seem to encourage men to do the same, and yet men would also profit emotionally from having a group of close male friends with whom they could share activities and conversation.

I remember my grandfather meeting other men at the old general store on a daily basis. I am not at all sure what it was that they discussed, but the custom surely filled a basic social need. It would appear that older men in our society would profit from a coffee shop type of establishment that encouraged such activities as card playing, checkers or chess.

There are some group activities that seem to appeal to retired men. Habitat for Humanity is one of them. Men seem to enjoy working together on this quite valuable social project. I also know of some retired men who organized a support group to renovate a very old water-powered mill. It not only utilized their many skills, it provided an excellent social situation. I heard of another couple who organized a group of gardeners, and spent each summer designing, planting, and caring for a number of flower gardens in their Midwestern city.

Such activities not only benefit the communities involved, but they provide social interaction, and also give the individuals a sense of accomplishment.

9
MENTOR
OCTOBER, 1996

There is general agreement in our present society that our children are lacking positive role models. With both parents working, children spend less time with their parents. With grandparents healthier and more mobile, they are also less likely to spend much time with their grandparents.

Big Brother and Big Sister programs are helping fill the needs some children are experiencing. Other kinds of mentoring programs are also proving valuable. Since older men represent an enormous reservoir of experience, skills, and wisdom, society could profit greatly by developing structures that would encourage them to work with young boys on various projects.

A tree planted by a boy and his grandfather would benefit society a great deal more than a tree planted by either one of them alone. A fish caught by an old man and a boy is a duel experience and will certainly taste better if they share the meal. A ball game attended by a three generation span adds a dimension to the game that far exceeds the actual score.

It was with my grandfather, walking in the woods, that I learned the difference between a walnut tree and a hickory nut tree, a gooseberry and a blackberry, a wren and catbird, and why walking in the woods was so special.

It's not so much the facts that a boy can learn from an old man. It's the perspective. It's an antidote for the young boy's passion for immediate gratification. And the old man learns from the boy that dreams and endless enthusiasm are born anew with each generation. As they nurture each other they realize that any moment can last forever if it is shared.

To be a successful mentor, one must learn to listen carefully. Until one understands the needs of the person being mentored no real progress will be accomplished. A mentor is not a preacher. A mentor is a companion. Young people learn best by sharing a project with an older, more experienced person.

Mentoring is teaching by example. It may not be giving advice at all. First of all, very few people welcome advice they did not ask for. However, they can choose to follow an example without losing face.

Young people today are bombarded by facts on a daily basis. However, due partly to our high divorce rate, they have little opportunity to share positive time with a caring adult. Never has our younger generation needed mentors as critically as they do today.

There are mentoring opportunities in our Boys and Girls Club programs. There is also a need for volunteers in our schools. Adults who listen to children read are mentoring if in no other way than by their demonstrating how important they consider reading to be. Sunday schools teachers are also mentoring by teaching what they consider are basic moral principles. Anytime we demonstrate by our behavior how important we consider something to be, we are mentoring.

10
CHILDREN
NOVEMBER, 1996

Related to shared experiences, is the problem a retired person must face in trying to decide whether or not to support their children or grandchildren physically, emotionally or financially when such support is either requested or seems appropriate.

Support can be detrimental if it robs the recipient of a personal feeling of accomplishment. Support can also be negative if it is not desired. It is definitely undesirable if the developing person becomes dependent on the support, and consequently fails to become a self-supporting person. Even though it's difficult to watch a loved one suffer, unneeded support can "save" a person from the hardship experiences that tend to strengthen a person's character and insure continuing success.

However, there are many occasions when emotional support is invaluable in helping a person through difficult times. There are also circumstances where an experienced helping hand can make the completion of a task possible. When it comes to financial support, the decision is more complicated. It does seem to be more satisfactory in the case of financial support, if the transaction is kept on a strictly business level.

Whatever the decision concerning support, one thing is certain. The support needs to be unconditional. You cannot offer your emotional support on the condition that your son makes the career decision that you consider appropriate. You cannot offer to pay for your daughter's wedding only if she marries a young man of whom you approve. You cannot offer to babysit grandchildren on the condition that you decide on how they are to be raised. Conditional support is not only a violation of another person's rights, but, more important, it doesn't work.

Unconditional support is based on unconditional love. Such love involves the complete giving of one's self to another person to use in a given circumstance as they see fit. It's very difficult to leave oneself so vulnerable, but the alternative is a holding back that just doesn't quite get the job done.

The most difficult part of parenting is supporting a child's first attempts at decision making. It's important for a child to have numerous experiences in the decision making process. However their first attempts will be based on very little information, and very little experience. A parent still must support their right as an individual to make their own decisions.

More important, they must be held responsible for the consequences of their decisions. Parents should neither deny them the opportunities to make decisions, or bail them out of the consequences when the decision is unwise. If they are never allowed to suffer the consequences of a poor decision, they will never develop the habit of trying to anticipate the consequences of a decision before they make it.

11
FOCUSING
NOVEMBER, 1996

As one becomes older it seems to be common for a person to spend more and more time alone, either by choice or by force of circumstances. Consequently, thinking about one's own needs rather than the needs of others appears to occur naturally. A simultaneous concern with one's self rather than one's environment seems to accelerate.

This focusing inward rather than outward leads not only to unhappiness, but to an unhealthy kind of aging. It shrinks the personality rather than expanding it. In order to be healthy, a person's body needs dependable, appropriate routine. In contrast, in order for our mind to be healthy, it needs dependable, appropriate variety. Concentrating on one's self constitutes a deadly kind of sameness which effectively starves the mind over a period of time. However, focusing on other's needs and on our environment, supplies an infinite variety of physical and emotional experiences.

This explains why the retiree who volunteers his time and energy to his community is a happier person than one who spends all his time and energy on himself.

There is another benefit derived from concentrating on others' needs rather than on one's own. Our self concept is developed as a result of our experiences. If we only do those things that satisfy our own needs, our experiences are quite limited. If we agree to do the variety of tasks necessary to fill the needs of others, our experiences become quite varied; the more variable our experiences, the more accurate our self concept. It is also true that the more accurate our self concept, the better our chance for happiness.

Many men of my generation spent a lifetime doing routine work. The need to support a family denied us the opportunity of doing a great variety of activities. Consequently, we never really became familiar with the many facets of our personalities. The freedom to experiment that retirement offers us should not be ignored. It is never too late to experience the delight of discovering something new about our own potential.

It does take courage to try something new as one becomes older. However, the alternative is to stop growing. It also takes energy that we might not have as much of as we once had. Working with and for other persons does seem to spark our interest and stoke our energy level more than working alone on our own needs. We also learn from other people. Their example and encouragement can help us discover our own hidden potential in a most enjoyable way.

There are many adult classes being offered in most communities at this time. Their popularity reflects the growing desire by adults to explore fields they have never had the opportunity to learn about. They are finding that as they increase their knowledge of their environment, they are also increasing their knowledge of themselves.

12
PROCRASTINATION
FEBRUARY, 1997

If you have been a lifetime procrastinator, then retirement presents you with a definite problem. Having a seemingly infinite number of empty tomorrows to count on, you really don't have to do anything today. It can always be done tomorrow. Consequently, you may find yourself unable to start anything.

Procrastination (not doing something until you absolutely have to) is the opposite of doing something as soon as possible. We always have the choice of either procrastinating or of expediting a task. We can identify readily with someone saying, "I'll do it later," but we rarely hear someone saying, 'I'll do it now."

Reasons why we may procrastinate:
1. Getting started is the hardest part of any task.
2. We are doing something else at the moment that we would much rather do.
3. The task consists of things we really dislike doing.
4. We are not in the right mood for this particular task.
5. Maybe if we wait, we won't have to do it at all.

Reasons why we may decide to expedite a task:
1. We want to get it, or someone, off our back.
2. We have the time to do it today, and we may not have the time tomorrow.

3. If we start it now, we will more likely have enough time to do the task well.
4. We really enjoy doing this kind of task, and we can't wait to get started.

But why are some people habitual procrastinators and other people habitual expediters, regardless of the circumstances? Is this a personality characteristic from birth or a behavioral pattern that we develop?

I believe that it is a behavioral pattern over which we have as much control as any other aspect of our behavior. I also believe that the expediters among us have a distinct advantage over the procrastinators in living their daily lives.

So how do we become an expediter? Assuming you really want to, your first step is to keep a running list of tasks. A task is placed on your list only if it is something you really want to do, or it is something that you are reasonably sure you will eventually have to do. Carrying a 3x5 card and a pen makes keeping the list quite convenient.

Check your list at least once a day, and mentally commit a given task to a given time. Prioritizing the list is not nearly as important as assigning a task to an appropriate time. However, most important of all is to remove something from the list each day by completing one or more tasks.

Expediters accomplish much more than procrastinators, and yet they have more time to play. The reason this is true is because procrastinators waste a great deal of time avoiding their tasks. This is neither a pleasurable or efficient use of time. Expediters, however, not only have more time to play, they are able to play, free of worry about meeting a deadline.

Because procrastinators wait until the very last minute to complete a task, they effectively allow the people who set the deadlines to control their lives. They also place themselves in the precarious position of having to estimate accurately the amount of time that a specific task will require for completion.

In contrast, expediters, by scheduling their time to complete a task as soon as possible, not only have plenty of time to do the task well, but effectively succeed in being in control of their own lives.

13
VOLUNTEERS
OCTOBER, 1997

Our society depends more every day on volunteers; those people who, for one reason or another, are willing to give of their time and talents to help someone else reach a goal. They are also willing to do this without pay. Most non-profit groups rely on volunteers to get the job done, and they are successful only to the extent that they are able to coordinate their volunteers' efforts effectively over a significant period of time.

If you are ever in a position where you are coordinating the efforts of a group of volunteers, remember that you are a coordinator, not a supervisor. Supervisors tell people what to do and pay them money for doing it. A coordinator carefully explains the group's ultimate goal, lists in detail the tasks that must be accomplished to reach that goal, and then allows individual volunteers to choose the tasks with which they feel most comfortable.

It is at this point that many coordinators become frustrated when their volunteers do not step forward and choose a task. Actually the word, volunteer, is a bit misleading. Many fine volunteers prefer to be personally asked to work at a given task. Their non-assertive personalities are such that they do not feel comfortable stepping forward and saying, "I'll do that." Therefore, the coordinator must know his or her volunteers well enough to ask the right person to do the right task.

Furthermore, once the coordinator has agreed that a given

volunteer is the one responsible to complete a given task, that volunteer must be given the necessary authority to accomplish that task in whatever manner he or she sees fit. Advice or help is provided by the coordinator only if it is requested by the volunteer.

An effective coordinator also makes personal contact with each volunteer on a regular basis. Appropriate times to do this are when recruiting a volunteer, when delegating a task, when responding to a request for advice or help, or when a volunteer has completed a task and deserves congratulations.

It is true that volunteers work hard for no money. However, they will continue to work only if they receive a feeling of accomplishment. It is your main job, as coordinator, to see to it that they do. If you have a specific, well-defined goal, match your volunteers' talents to the appropriate tasks, respond readily to requests for advice and help, and give recognition for a job well done, you will succeed in helping your volunteers achieve a feeling of accomplishment.

Volunteers also can be frustrated by more than one coordinator. Committees do not make good coordinators. It seems to be most effective to have only one coordinator for any one goal.

In conclusion, remember that there is no limit to what a group of well-coordinated volunteers can accomplish.

Philip, thank you for your order! Your order number is 90048816

Order Summary

Subtotal	$115.00
Shipping & processing	$12.95
Tax	$0.00
Total	**$127.95**

Order Number:90048816

Shipping to:

Philip Roberts

247 E. Flagg St.
PMB 372
Walcott, IA 52773-7737

Method:Standard Shipping (3 - 6 business days)

Description	Quantity	Order total:
Truly Me™ Doll: Light Skin with Freckles, Curly Blond Hair, Blue Eyes	1	$115.00

Need Help?

FAQs   Shipping information   Contact us

14
RETURNS
DECEMBER, 1997

Frequently, we read in the newspaper about some person being the victim of a scam artist. Usually it is an older person. We have even coined the phrase, "If it seems too good to be true, it probably is." Yet, we all like to get the best possible return on our investment. However, it's unrealistic to expect o get something for nothing. Every return requires some kind of investment.

I like searching for morel mushrooms in the spring because it requires only an investment of my time. Hunting and fishing requires a license and special equipment, but the return for the hunter and fisherman can be worth considerably more than the investment. However, with mushrooms, fish, or game, the return might instead be nothing, depending on one's skill.

The stock market is one of the more famous investments, and again your return depends on one's knowledge and ability. Yet there could be a market crash and no return, or even considerable loss.

When gambling with slot machines, cards, or dice, one is playing the odds, and luck plays a great part in whether or not there is a return or an outright loss. There can be a big return. There can also be big loss. The gambler is never in complete control. But the gambler is intrigued by the immediate response. In fact, the immediate response of the slot machine is probably its greatest appeal for the gambler.

Actually, we are all gamblers as we make many daily choices in our on-going lives. But by demanding immediate gratification, we limit our choices. This is one of the reasons that people who can afford to leave their money invested in long term investments are the ones who have the best returns.

Great gardeners are some of the most successful gamblers in the world. However, to be a great gardener one must plan carefully over a long period of time and be very patient. From a small seed one can reap a big return if enough planning and patience is employed. Gardening is my favorite form of investing. With a large investment of time and energy, and a small financial investment, my return borders at times on the miraculous.

However, immediate gratification is impossible. Planning the garden in January, poring over the seed catalogs in February, pricking out the seedlings in March, preparing the soil in April, planting the plants in May, then the weeding, watering, and waiting, is followed finally by the big return: a veritable kaleidoscope of flowers and produce.

Some people consider gambling a very undesirable activity. Those same people gamble on a daily basis with their health by smoking, or drinking alcohol in excess. Most of us take chances daily by exceeding the speed limit.

It isn't whether or not one gambles. Our concern should be how much we are risking when we gamble, and whether or not it's what we can afford to lose.

15
PROJECTS
OCTOBER, 1998

It would appear that retirement is as exciting as we make it. Aside from a healthy daily routine, people seem to be happiest when they are working on a project. It might be a trip. It might be a garden. It might be a quilt. It might be painting the house. Succeeding on the projects is, of course, important. The difference between completing a project and not completing it is the difference between feeling like a winner, and feeling like a loser.

I think five things are essential to successful completion of a project. They are health, time, opportunity, motivation, and support.

Poor physical health can prevent a person from reaching a goal. One has a tendency to concentrate on one's self when ill. To reach a goal, it is necessary to concentrate on each objective that attains the goal. Poor physical health can also make reaching a goal actually impossible if the process requires a great deal of stamina and perseverance. Maintaining a high level of physical health can prevent one's missing an opportunity that may occur only once in a lifetime.

It takes a certain amount of one's time to reach any goal. In this respect, the retired person has an advantage, if they have learned to manage their time wisely. They also have to be willing and able to give up time-consuming activities of questionable importance. Prioritizing is a necessity if one is to find sufficient time to reach a new goal. Allotting ample time to reach a goal is usually the wisest approach. Doing so allows time for careful planning. In the long run, careful planning prevents mistakes, and therefore actually saves time.

A person can be in excellent health, and have ample time, but if the opportunity doesn't present itself, they won't reach their goal. The weather might prevent a person from mowing the lawn. Lack of money to buy supplies might prevent a person from redecorating a room. Sometimes we can create an opportunity, and sometimes it is beyond our control. It helps to have money in savings. It also helps to remain alert and well-informed. Sometimes we miss opportunities because we don't have the resources available to take advantage of them. Other times we miss opportunities because we don't know that they exist.

Very few things are as important as the enthusiasm one brings to a project. It's not only important to be genuinely excited about starting a project; one must maintain a high level of motivation in order to complete a quality job. Planning and careful research can increase a person's level of interest. The more we know about what we are doing, the more interesting it is. Physical health is actually improved by the excitement of anticipation. Our overall quality of life depends on our having something positive to look forward to each day.

Frequently, we try to "go it alone." However, even when we do, we are relying on considerable support to achieve our goal, whether we realize it or not. Support comes in many forms. It might be a friend saying, "I know you can do it." It might be a family member offering to help finance the project. It could be a helpful librarian who directs us to just the right information. I might be a neighbor who offers to do one of our routine chores for us so we can have the needed, uninterrupted time. Learn to accept support graciously. Many persons, who would never attempt a project of their own, derive considerable satisfaction out of helping someone else.

16
GRIEF
NOVEMBER, 1998

Whenever a person suffers a significant loss, they seem to experience five stages of grief: Denial, Anger, Bargaining, Depression, and Acceptance.

I am convinced that few people, who have not experienced it, understand the severe loss suffered by a person who has just retired. Retirement involves a loss of friends, a loss of identity, and even a loss of one's lifestyle.

At first, it's hard to believe that it is actually happening. Consequently, one experiences denial; a refusal to admit that anything is really happening, so some people just go get another job, refusing to join the ranks of the unemployed. They cannot conceive of a lifestyle that doesn't include going to work on a daily basis. This kind of person will probably die on the job and do so happily. However, most people do eventually retire because they have no practical alternative.

Many persons become intensely angry shortly after realizing that retirement is actually taking place. When this happens, it helps to understand that anger is a symptom of fear, frustration or disappointment. If one can determine which of the three is most prevalent, the anger is easier to deal with.

Once a person's anger has subsided, he might decide to look for ways to soften the shock of being retired. He may offer to be a part-time consultant for the people taking his place. They could logically profit from his years of experience. Or possibly he could volunteer to help out as a sub. This kind of bargaining rarely helps solve the problem of not accepting the reality of retirement. But it may help distract the anger.

When bargaining fails to help, depression can occur. Depression constitutes a loss of hope in the future. Depression can even negatively affect one's physical health. Consequently this is the point at which some men begin to die. Physical activity of any kind helps treat depression. Drugs treat the symptom; feeling depressed. Physical activity treats the cause: a feeling of no value. Anything that will give a person a sense of accomplishment, and therefore a feeling of worth will help them move on to the fifth stage.

And finally comes acceptance; a realization that you have started a new life. A new life that will not include going to work on a daily basis, but a new life that can include meaningful activity, or a new life that may be more fulfilling than anything you have ever experienced before.

The grief process is not an optional experience. It is a natural, automatic process that allows us to give up a core dream, and move on to what is now true, as opposed to what was. It takes time to work ourselves through the process. It involves examining and discarding much of our old life style, and developing a new one. No one really enjoys change, especially as they age. Our job is to work through the change carefully and move on to a new life.

17
IMAGE
NOVEMBER, 1998

Not only does a man's self image suffer from retirement, his public image is immediately associated with the "Dirty Old Man" syndrome. An old man walking alone in a park is suspect. A grandfather is not afforded the opportunity to baby-sit the way a grandmother is. Unless he is well-groomed, it is assumed that an old man is a bum. If he tells an off-color joke, he is a pervert. Such irrational assumptions, just because a man is old, can be very frustrating.

It is worth a retired man's time to work hard on this public image. Good grooming is the first step. It takes time, but then that is the one thing a retired man should feel free to use in any way he sees fit. A daily morning shower and shave is basic, unless a man prefers a well-trimmed beard. Good, clean, serviceable clothing is worth the investment. When white collar workers retire, they should seriously consider trying some quality work clothes. My favorite pair of shoes now is a pair of work shoes that I bought at a farm store. Quality jeans are not only comfortable, but they present a neat appearance. Good sweatshirts can be expensive, but they are also very comfortable and can last a long time.

As for the "Dirty" in "Dirty Old Man," it might be worth our time to clean up our language and never tell another dirty joke. Sex may be a legitimate part of our private life, but no one seems to be able to handle it being part of our public life.

For some strange reason, old men are also assumed to be self-centered. This is an image we can do something about. Spontaneous and regular acts of kindness will convince people that even an old man can be thoughtful and unselfish. I remember an older neighbor who walked his neighbors' dogs when the owners were no longer able to do so. He also made frequent trips to the neighborhood grocery store for those same neighbors.

Remembering friends and relatives' birthdays need not be time-consuming or expensive. A simple card would be greatly appreciated. If you see an empty cart outside the grocery store, take it in with you. In doing so you will be making someone's job just a little lighter.

I have another senior neighbor who owns a snow blower. He generously cleans the street sidewalk for our entire block. Such positive contact with his neighborhood helps a retired person keep in touch with other people on a positive note. Even a "Dirty Old Man" wants to be liked.

My grandfather tended a large garden every summer up until the day he died. He and grandmother couldn't possibly begin to use all of the produce he raised. Consequently, he spent many hours harvesting the vegetables and distributing them to neighbors who had no gardens.

As I look back, I realize that my grandparents had very little wealth. Regardless, my grandfather was looked upon by his neighbors as a very generous man.

18
ALONE
DECEMBER, 1998

One of the changes occurring after retirement is in the amount of time a person spends alone. Typically, one's children are living independently. If one's spouse is also still working a full or part-time job, a man will find himself spending a great deal of time alone.

Most people enjoy having some time alone. They need solitary time to relax, think, work out problems, or just enjoy a solitary pleasure. However, typical men have had little time for themselves when they worked every day, and then came home in the evening to their families. Not having had much time alone, they have had little experience in how to use it wisely.

Some people thoroughly enjoy solitary activities such as reading or writing. I have found gardening very enjoyable. My brother loves golf, whether or not he's alone. I have friends who can spend many hours playing gambling machines by themselves. However, few people like to eat alone or attend social events alone. Some people like to travel alone, but most would prefer a companion.

A man might find that, if his wife had always been primarily a homemaker, she still prefers to spend much of her day alone. His presence, after retirement, can be a source of considerable irritation. It doesn't mean that she no longer loves him. It just means that she has become use to enjoying her time alone and misses it.

A man's first shock, when he finds himself with much time alone, is the realization that he seems to be stuck with a rather dull companion. This might be an excellent time for a man to learn more about himself. One can only do this through a variety of experiences. No one is dull by nature. Dullness comes from living in a rut.

The man with the courage and the ambition to search out and experience new things will discover that having an abundance of unscheduled time available can help one develop an exciting lifestyle.

Trying something new is less socially intimidating if you can join someone you know who is already doing it. If you need training and can find a community college class that offers what you want to learn, you will also find that the class will afford you the opportunity to meet new people. Because you're in the same class you will probably have some things in common.

Annual city events need volunteers to help conduct them successfully. These events not only can be another opportunity to meet new people, but also a chance to try something for a very short commitment to see if you enjoy it.

You won't enjoy everything you try, but if you don't give up, you will find activities that help you discover not only some new things you enjoy, but also talents you might never have known that you possess.

19
CONTROL
DECEMBER, 1998

Psychologists frequently tell people to take control of their own lives. This is generally good advice, but many of us have had little opportunity to actually do so. As a child, our parents controlled our lives. If a man was in the military, he remembers having little or no control over his own life. When one marries and starts a family, the needs of the family dictate how a man spends most of his time.

Retirement, however, provides a true opportunity for a person to take control of his own life. It might be difficult, because there are always people around who like to manipulate other people. It might be a son or daughter. It might be a spouse. It could easily be an aging parent. It's important to realize that if you don't make your own decisions there will always be somebody else willing to make them for you.

Start by forcing yourself to plan ahead. Don't go to bed without thinking seriously about how you plan to spend the next day. It's very important for a retired person to keep some kind of a calendar. Its purpose is to remind you of the things that you want to do. First, list those things that you truly enjoy. Then set aside specific times for doing them. When someone asks you to do something that you detest doing, it feels good to be able to truthfully say, "I'm sorry but I planned to do something else at that time."

Happiness is joyfully anticipating tomorrow. Having something to look forward to, improves your chances of being happy. Planning makes all of this possible. Taking control of your life requires successful planning.

I find it necessary to carry a three-by-five card and a pen at all times. Each Sunday I make a list of all the things I must do the following week, and of all of the things I want to do. Unless I make this list on a regular basis and specify when I am going to do each thing, I am likely to forget something important to me in the rush of everyday activities.

I might choose to do something different from what I have planned if something more interesting comes up. And, of course, there are emergencies. However, the plan gives me a sense of direction, which is difficult to maintain when one has unlimited free time.

I also find that I can accomplish a great deal more if I plan carefully. I have learned, in addition, that I am much happier if I can feel a sense of accomplishment on a regular basis. To feel a sense of accomplishment I don't need to do anything of any great importance to anyone else. It just needs to be something I have considered important enough to me to be placed on my list. It might be something as unimportant as clipping my toenails. It might be mowing the lawn. It might also be visiting a friend who is house-bound.

20
FUN
DECEMBER, 1998

Many people are so busy during their regular working years that the aspect of retirement that appeals to them most is the luxury of being able to do nothing. During the years when you would give anything to have some free time, it is inconceivable that having nothing to do would be unbearably boring, but it is.

We also remember the fun times being always too short. There was never enough vacation time to really enjoy the trip or whatever it was that we had planned to do. Therefore, one important part of retirement was definitely going to be pleasure without interruptions.

The problem with fun turns out to be that for many people, working was their greatest source of pleasure. They now must discover what activities there are that they can also enjoy. In doing this they must keep in mind certain criteria. It has to be an activity that they can afford. Maybe they have always wanted to delve into photography. Unless their photos can generate some income, this can be an expensive pastime. It may be they truly enjoy gambling. If they live close to a casino (I live five minutes from a riverboat casino), they must consider what they can afford to lose and still maintain their lifestyle. If a person just enjoys playing cards (without gambling), and can find a group that does so regularly, there need not be any financial consideration. Gardening is an activity that can be as inexpensive or expensive as a person wants to make it.

Once a person finds something that they enjoy, that they also can afford, they must consider how it affects their health. A person might enjoy dining out. If they do so regularly, they would have to consider their choice of food carefully to remain healthy. Or one could get a great deal of pleasure from working out in a gym. This could be a fine activity, if not overdone.

In fact, moderation in pleasurable activities seems to be a requirement if the pleasure is going to last, and if the activity is not going to be detrimental. Too much of anything dulls the pleasure and creates problems. A good motto seems to be, "Quit while you're still having fun." Therefore, it would seem that a person needs a wide variety of pleasurable activities to truly enjoy a large amount of free time. Constant experimentation is one answer. Trying new activities when one is older may be intimidating. Many seniors assume, because they are older, that they won't be able to learn how to do something new. We have no way of knowing, no matter our age, whether or not we can do something we have never tried. However it takes courage and considerable effort to try new activities for the first time when you're seventy. Yet, you just might discover something at seventy that gives you twenty years of intense pleasure.

21
SEX
JANUARY, 1999

And what about sex? The physical activity of sex, specifically intercourse, is obviously designed primarily for the young and vigorous. Their ample supply of both physical and emotional energy is ideally suited for sex. As for a person of my age, sex seems to be an extravagant, rather wasteful use of my energy when there are so many other things that bring me pleasure. Now that I have the time to savor the sunset and mellow out in the moonlight, sex pales in comparison to these as a source of sheer joy.

Then there is the primary purpose of intercourse; the creation of children. I think a person my age would have to be incredibly selfish to produce a child when they no longer have the energy to rear the child properly. They may not even have sufficient years remaining to complete the task.

I realize that everyone needs to be touched, hugged and caressed, regardless of age, in order to feel loved. But this is not sex. It is emotional support; something everyone needs and is capable of giving as long as they are alive.

Sexual intercourse, however, is like playing basketball or climbing a mountain. The typical person, who enjoyed them when they were younger, wisely leaves them behind as their amount of energy diminishes with age. For practical reasons they move on to other activities, just as pleasurable, but ones that require considerably less energy.

Our present society, with its inordinate emphasis on sex, gives one the impression that no pleasure compares to sex. We also are told that, if sex isn't one of our greatest pleasures in life, we have a problem. The media, which uses sex to promote products, has caused many of our societal problems. Even our high divorce rate is at least partially due to the unrealistically high expectations many young people have concerning sexual activity during marriage.

There is even considerable being written about older people enjoying sex as much as ever. And, if they physically can't, we have developed medication to make it possible. Instead of seeking other sources of pleasure, and other ways of expressing our intimacy we cling to an activity that is not necessarily appropriate for our physical condition.

Such an attitude toward sex has created numerous problems for our society. There is no logical reason for an older person to feel cheated if sex is not one of the great pleasures in their day-to-day life style. They could very possibly find something else at seventy that proves more deeply enjoyable for them than sex had ever been. Such a revelation should be met with joy, not a feeling that one has a problem.

22
PETS
JANUARY, 1999

Pets can be a great source of comfort for an older person, especially if the person is living alone. A pet can mean companionship, or even protection. Such a situation has many positive aspects.

However, retired persons frequently find themselves in a less desirable situation. The pets were acquired for the children. When the children mature, marry, and leave home, they leave the aging pets behind to be cared for by their aging parents.

This is not a happy combination. By definition, a pet is meant to enhance one's quality of life. An incontinent cat certainly does not enhance one's quality of life. An aging dog that can no longer tolerate a grandchild's antics becomes a menace rather than a protector. This is the situation that we faced shortly after our last child had left home. It was my responsibility to take the pets to the veterinarian to be put down. I was crying so hard that I could barely see to drive. It was a miserable job, but it had to be done.

When the retired person decides that euthanasia is a practical, compassionate solution for the pet problem, grown children frequently object. They are in no position to care for the pet that made their childhood so enjoyable. They may not even be able to see the pet more than two or three times a year. Never the less, they don't want to come back home and find the pet gone.

I remember having a St. Bernard dog as my pet on the farm. He was a very large, lovable, friendly dog that I really liked a lot. But I graduated from high school, and got a job fifty miles from my parent's farm. I was able to visit them very infrequently. One day I came home and my dog was gone. First, they told me that he had run away. I was very suspicious of their story, and I was very unhappy. Finally, months later, they felt free to tell me the truth. They said my dog had started attacking the neighbor's sheep. I didn't want to believe what they told me, but I now realize that they had no choice but to get rid of my dog.

In such a situation, the retired person should feel free to do whatever will contribute most to their personal peace of mind. As stated before, pets are meant to enhance one's quality of life. When they no longer do so, one might feel sadness, but should feel no guilt or remorse for doing whatever seems most desirable.

Also, an aging pet can be in considerable pain. Allowing them to suffer indefinitely is not a compassionate solution. Euthanasia is.

23
TECHNOLOGY
JANUARY, 1999

In our modern technological society, the longer one lives the more difficult it is to keep up. Man has always had to cope with change. The problem now has been complicated because change is happening ever more rapidly. It would seem that every day brings some technological change that may affect anyone's lifestyle.

To resist change in our present culture, can mean jeopardizing our ability to communicate effectively. It can also mean wasting time and money. However, most changes are primarily for convenience.

It is more convenient to be able to shop while baking. One only needs to set the timer on a modern kitchen oven, and it will cook anything, at any temperature, at any time, while you are shopping. The modern furnace thermostat can be set so that it reduces your home's heat during certain hours, such as at night. Such a device saves money on utilities as well as being convenient.

Other advances might be more complicated. It seems we were just getting use to the TV and its remote control (definitely a convenience), when along comes the VCR. It is not only less expensive to rent a video than to go to a theater for a movie, but if you have grandchildren, you must learn to operate the VCR. Grandchildren not only visit their grandparents, they might decide to bring with them their favorite video. I don't believe that watching a movie is as positive an experience as helping their grandfather in the garden, but if they insist on a movie it helps to be able to operate the

VCR yourself. It will last longer if you do.

A cordless phone, which I didn't really think we needed, has become one of our favorite conveniences. Being able to just press a button for frequently called numbers that have been programmed in is great. The redial feature also saves time. The change to the cordless was a comparatively easy one to make.

And then they introduced the personal computer. Regardless of what your children or your grandchildren tell you, learning to effectively use a computer is not easy. I think a simpler first step would be to purchase a word processor. It costs a third to a fourth of what a computer costs and its functions are much easier to learn. They also prepare one to use a computer.

First, on a word processor, you learn how to use disks to store information. If you are just wishing to type a paper, you can first observe it for errors on the monitor screen. Learning to use the 'insert' function to correct your errors is not very difficult. Once the errors are corrected you can have the paper printed out. These functions are similar enough to those on a computer that they can be of considerable value when you make the transition.

If you purchase a computer, it is imperative that you arrange for detailed instruction on its use. Many businesses are selling computers without adequate instruction or follow up for their customers. This can be very frustrating for a beginner.

I don't know whether old dogs can learn new tricks of not. I do know that old men can, and if they want to be able to cope happily with modern society, they must not only learn new tricks, they need to become very adept at them.

24
PARENTS
JANUARY, 1999

When my mother died of a heart attack at the age of seventy-four on the way to a party, it was quite a shock for the family. We didn't realize at the time how lucky we all were. In contrast, I have a friend who is eighty-nine and she hasn't had a rational day in the last five years.

Medical science has become more and more adept at keeping the human body alive. However, psychiatry has made very little progress in postponing dementia. Caring for the aged after they are no longer capable of caring for themselves has become a major task for our society.

The extended family seems no longer able or willing to provide this care. Consequently, the nursing home business is continually expanding. Since the average retirement income is insufficient to pay for such extended care, the government will probably need to provide assistance in increasing amounts.

I have many retired friends whose major social responsibility is making sure that their aging parent is being adequately provided for. Even if they are able to find their parent a fine care facility, there are still many responsibilities to attend to. Someone must handle their finances. Someone must purchase their clothing. And someone must visit them on a regular basis so they won't feel abandoned. If you are the only child living in the same community as your parent, then these responsibilities will be yours.

Your parent saw that your needs were met when you were a baby. Now it is your turn to care for your parent who, in much the same condition, cannot possibly fulfill their own most basic needs.

I have a neighbor and his wife who have been married for seventy years. They are both in their early nineties and they are no longer allowed to drive a car. Public transportation in our community is quite inadequate. Since I live very close to them, I have been taking them with me to a euchre tournament twice a week. They are excellent euchre players, and I also enjoy the games a great deal. It gives them something to look forward to each week.

One might say that such entertainment would not be a basic necessity. However, for many older citizens, their social isolation is a worse problem than their physical condition.

Euthanasia is being considered as a solution for the aging problem by a significant portion of our society. I believe we would lose something very important if we ever agreed that euthanasia should be legalized. Caring for a helpless parent is a tedious, yet character building experience. It puts our inevitable vulnerability in proper perspective. It could very well be the most maturing experience you'll ever have.

25

TRAVELING

FEBRUARY, 1999

In spite of our grown children's misgivings, we took a five thousand mile camping trip last summer. They didn't think that we could take care of ourselves, and they were also worried about our thirteen year-old car which had already gone one hundred seventy-four thousand miles. Actually, our beautiful old tent and our well cared for old Oldsmobile both came through with flying colors. They took good care of us, and we enjoyed the trip immensely.

This was our first opportunity in forty years to take a camping trip without the kids. It was certainly worth the effort. However, we learned that camping isn't what it was forty years ago when we were taking the family. In some of the campgrounds, we were the only campers with a tent. Everyone else had some kind of huge recreational vehicle. Consequently, the friendly camping conversations with other campers, that we used to enjoy so much, are no longer common.

I'll have to admit that as far as I am concerned, "RV camping" is an oxymoron. But then maybe that is sour grapes on my part since I couldn't possibly afford one. There are now retired people buying RVs and calling them home. I couldn't do that, because I need roots for a feeling of security, but some people find it to be an ideal lifestyle. However, it is not traveling. It is a nomadic lifestyle. In contrast, traveling is a break from a more routine lifestyle.

When traveling, it makes a trip more enjoyable if it is well planned.

Traveling also takes a lot of energy, especially if you want to escape the crowds and get close to nature. We have discovered that if one is willing to hike, even a short distance, it's easy to escape the crowds.

Any retired person has the time and resources to travel if it appeals to him. It would seem that the ones who enjoy traveling the most, however, travel light (maybe one small suitcase), and refuse to waste any energy worrying about specific deadlines or destinations. Retired persons have the time flexibility that allows them to ignore schedule difficulties while traveling.

My wife found a trip with the computer's aid. It was a package one had to commit to months ahead of time. It included round trip air fare from Chicago to Rome, plus six nights at a centrally located hotel in the heart of the city. It also included transportation to and from the airport and the hotel. This was all for a very modest fee. We were entirely on our own and thoroughly enjoyed wandering the streets of Rome for six days. This kind of trip costs one-third to one-fourth the cost of a guided tour. As long as one is physically and mentally healthy, this method of traveling could prove to be a desirable alternative for one on a limited budget.

Traveling, admittedly, takes a great deal of effort. However, I find it intellectually quite stimulating. I never feel the same about a location once I have physically been there.

26
TIME
SEPTEMBER, 1999

Time can weigh heavily on a retired person's hands, or it can become one of his most valuable assets. However, a retired person needs to develop a new concept of time to enjoy its benefits to the fullest. It helps to assume, first of all, that you have an unlimited amount of time to accomplish anything you wish to start. Rushing is not only irrational during retirement; it is in conflict with one's diminishing energy level.

Once a person accepts the unlimited time concept, various facts become clear: There is time for careful planning before starting a job. You have time to savor each step of the job. You can spend as much time on details as you wish. The job does not have to be finished today. If you get tired, you can take a nap. If the finished job is not what you intended, you can do it over.

At seventy, I decided one summer to reroof and paint my garage. My children, genuinely worried, tried to dissuade me from doing it. I assured them that I had the time and the experience to do the job, and if I ran out of energy and needed help I would ask for it. Removing the three layers of old roofing was a dirty, time consuming task that required patience and four trips to the landfill. Putting on the new roof was more enjoyable. Repairing rotted wood and painting the garage took a great deal of time, even though my wife helped paint. She not only enjoys painting, but is much better on the trim jobs that I. My son-in-law also helped me with some of the more strenuous parts of the job.

So the garage took all summer. Time was not important. The fact that my doing the work saved me considerable cash, kept me healthy, and gave me a real sense of accomplishment was important.

Jobs I used to do in an hour, when I could find the time, are now allotted a half day. Jobs that I used to do in a day are now accomplished in a week. The tasks are now much more enjoyable, and the finished product has a greatly enhanced quality. Such quality work also gives one a greater sense of accomplishment.

Unlimited time gives you the opportunity to arrive early for every appointment, eliminating traffic problems and avoiding the consequences of unexpected delays. I now read the entire newspaper every morning over breakfast. I might even start writing letters, since I seem to frequently forget what I want to say when I am using the phone.

People complain about our Iowa weather. Now that I have flexible time I can enjoy the sunny day even if it falls on a Monday. I have other activities that I save for the rainy days. Learning to turn the ample, flexible time one has in retirement into an asset rather than a liability seems to be a basic skill needed for happy retirement.

27
CONVERSATION
OCTOBER, 1999

We old men are rarely thought of as good conversationalists. The problem seems to be our compulsion to tell our story rather than listen to someone else's. The fact that we might have many good stories to tell is irrelevant. Good conversation must include good listening.

I thought I was a good listener until I caught myself one day mentally planning my story while my friend was telling his. If you've lived seventy years, it's not difficult to top anyone's story. In an attempt to become a better listener, I have decided that anytime I catch myself thinking about what I want to say while someone else is talking, I will deny myself the pleasure of telling my story. It's quite egotistical to expect someone to want to listen to your story when you're not interested in listening to theirs.

We also have the tendency to repeat a story that our friends have heard numerous times before. No story is that good. We owe it to our friends and especially to our close family members to let the old stories die. If you want to preserve them, write them down.

Listening well is a very difficult skill to develop. It not only means ignoring what you want to say, it means actually ignoring yourself so that you can experience what the other person is feeling as he talks.

A personally positive result of learning to listen well is the education we receive. My father once told me when I was ridiculing an uneducated neighbor, "If you listen carefully, you can learn something from anyone. This is true because, no matter whom you are talking with, they know some things that you do not."

Listening has another advantage. By listening, especially to younger persons, an older man keeps in touch with the present. In contrast, telling old stories has a tendency to encourage him to live in the past. It is only in the present that a man will be able to live a meaningful and enjoyable retirement.

Conversation is a major source of pleasure for older men. Many small communities have a restaurant where local retired men meet each morning for coffee and conversation. They discuss local and international problems, sharing their opinions while enjoying the social interchange. Some larger cities have neighborhood meeting places for the older people, but many do not.

Older foreign countries have their famous coffee shops where older people sit around and discuss the world's problems, or maybe play a game of chess. I believe as our country has more and more older people, we might also develop meeting places comparable to those in older cultures.

28
EXERCISE
NOVEMBER, 1999

I helped my wife clean house the other day. I now know why women generally outlive men. The exercise they get cleaning house would alone be significant enough to make the difference.

In fact, it appears that women get an increasing amount of exercise in relation to their energy level as they get older, while men get less and less exercise in relation to their energy level as they get older. I believe this is a direct result of men spending their lives developing and using labor-saving devices in order to work more efficiently. To be healthy retired men, we must reverse this process.

Instead of a riding mower, we should be using one that requires as much physical energy as we can muster and still get the job done. Once you are retired, time should no longer be a factor. There are a number of other things we could do that would also take advantage of our ample available time, and provide more exercise in the process.

When parking in a large parking lot, as at a shopping mall, we should park in the first space that we come to, disregarding how far we might have to walk to get to the mall entrance. Walking is excellent exercise. Such an approach to parking would also be far less stressful than the frustration we experience in not being able to find a close parking spot.

Depending on how many flights of stairs a man has to climb to reach his destination, he should not use the elevator. It is just another device invented to save time and energy. Unless you are handicapped in some way, climbing the stairs would provide good exercise.

For gardeners, spading is hard work. The tiller was invented to make the job a lot easier. However, tilling doesn't work the soil deep enough to do a good job of preparing flower beds. Spading is not only better for the plants; it is better exercise for the gardener.

Also for gardeners, we have developed numerous chemicals to kill weeds. Pulling weeds by hand is hard work, but it is fine exercise. We are also becoming aware of the fact that the chemicals are environmentally destructive. In fact, many labor-saving devices are environmentally undesirable.

The automobile is a classic example. We should consciously ask ourselves, when time is not relevant, if we could walk to our destination without using the car. If we are only purchasing one or two items, for example, that could easily be carried; the trip might just as well be a healthy walk rather than just another ride.

More and more communities are developing hiking and biking trails. If you are travelling, allow time to walk the trails. It's not only good exercise; it allows you to see a side of any community that you can't experience on the freeway or at the motel. You don't have to walk far to leave the crowds behind.

I just sacked up thirty bags of leaves yesterday. It was hard work and I slept well last night. While I was raking and sacking, my neighbor was using his new leaf blower. It is an impressive device with which he first blew the leaves into a pile. Then he reversed the mechanism and it sucked them up and shredded them before spitting them out. It is definitely a fine labor-saving device that helps in the composting process also. However, the extra exercise was good for me, and I had all day for the job.

29
MONEY
NOVEMBER, 1999

In our present society, the vast majority of retired people have sufficient income to meet their basic needs for food, clothing and shelter. However, since their income is limited, they are constantly forced to make choices. There are few retirees with enough money to buy everything they want, and to do everything they wish to do.

We are fortunate in our society that many choices are available. As for food, at one end of the spectrum we can garden and save considerable on the grocery bill. At the other end there are many fine restaurants available in most communities where once again we have choices available in a wide price range. Many persons make a healthy diet their first goal, and possibly eat out occasionally for entertainment.

As for clothing, the amount of money spent is very closely related to personal taste. Healthy, adequate clothing is also available in every price range. If one wishes, adequate clothing can be purchase in a used clothing store. Most communities also have the most exclusive shops. Our primary goal should be clean, comfortable clothing, appropriate for the weather and the occasion.

Shelter is a more complicated need. A house (such as our five-bedroom Victorian), which was ideal for raising five children, can become a maintenance burden as one gets older. A retired couple might prefer a much smaller home with no stairs. Or they might prefer a condominium with no maintenance required of them personally. And yet, some retired people want to maintain their own yard and garden as long as they can possibly do so.

Financially, many retired people have their homes paid for by the time they retire, and if their homes meet their retirement needs, they have no problem. Their only costs would be for utilities, property taxes, and maintenance.

Private transportation, although not absolutely essential, is certainly a desired convenience for most retired people as long as they are healthy enough to drive safely. Transportation vehicles also have a wide price range. There is a difference of thousands of dollars between the price of a ten-year-old car and a new one. Maintenance can also be expensive once a warranty has run its course. Unfortunately, public transportation is rarely convenient, depending on your city and your location.

Once a retired person has worked out a satisfactory budget to handle the necessities, he has one more decision regarding money. If he is in good health, he might be tempted to go back to work to provide extra spending money. Also, many retired persons are working, at least part time, because they just want something to fill up their unscheduled time. Others are working because they do want the extra money. It might be for a special trip or a new car. Whatever the reason, the person has to decide if it's worth giving up the freedom that comes with keeping time unscheduled.

The broad choice one makes between spending money on things and spending money on experiences is also a personal choice. Many retired persons have accumulated so many things that they hesitate to add to the clutter. However, if one prefers to spend his money on experiences, it will depend on his health and the appropriate experiences available. I have one neighbor who still loves to shop for antiques.

Regardless how one chooses to spend his retirement income, the choices are important. If one keeps accurate records of how he is spending his money it will help him make wise choices. He might discover that he can effectively have considerably more discretionary funds by simplifying his lifestyle. Such a decision might prove more satisfactory then going back to work.

30
BABYSITTING
DECEMBER, 1999

If you live in the same community as your grandchildren, occasionally you will be asked to babysit. This will give you an opportunity to get to know your grandchildren as they are growing up, and it could be a very positive experience. However, if you are asked to be a full-time caregiver while both parents work, it may not be a positive experience for you or your grandchildren.

Caring for your grandchildren eight hours a day or more, five days a week, requires you to play a very specific role. You are effectively raising your grandchildren in conjunction with their parents. This presents some very special problems.

Since you will have to be a regular disciplinarian, you will have little opportunity to play the traditional role of the indulgent grandparent. I have fond memories of my grandmother feeding me sweets that my mother would never have given me. I also remember my grandfather telling me stories that my father would never have had the time for. And I could confide in them in a way one cannot confide in one's disciplinarian. Therefore, as a fulltime caregiver, you are not only robbed of the pleasure of playing the grandparent role, your grandchildren are robbed of the pleasure of having genuine grandparents.

Another problem that may arise from a grandparent being a full-time care giver is due to the fact that the grandparent and the parent rarely agree on how a child should be raised. This conflict in rearing philosophy can not only cause friction between the adults, it can confuse the children.

The rules set down by the parents should naturally hold precedence over anyone else's rules. However, the grandparents could find this very frustrating if the parent's rules were inadequate to provide the kind of discipline that the grandparents believe appropriate. Different generations have a tendency to have different rules because each generation is trying to prepare their children for a different society than the previous one.

Many grandparents, depending on their health and age, will also find that they have insufficient energy to do a good job of taking care of children on a regular basis. They might especially find it emotionally exhausting. Grandparents may be asked to babysit because they seem to have lots of time. Also, it frequently saves the parent the considerable expense of hiring a babysitter.

Just because a grandparent seems to have a great deal of unscheduled time, doesn't mean they don't have a life. In fact, their choice of lifestyle may very well depend on ample unscheduled time. Whatever their reason, a grandparent should not feel obligated to say yes to full-time care giving of grandchildren, or feel guilty if they choose to say no.

31
GENEOLOGY
DECEMBER, 1999

I remember vividly the Memorial Day that my father insisted on taking the family to the old German cemetery where his grandparents were buried. We weren't all that interested at the time, but we respected our father sufficiently to humor his wishes.

It was forty years later when the wife of a distant cousin of mine in California wrote and asked me if I knew anything about her husband's ancestors. She was delighted to learn where they were buried. I was also able to give her the name of the old country church where records still existed. She was involved in doing extensive genealogical research on her husband's ancestors who also happened to be mine.

I profited greatly from the letters she sent me cataloging her findings. In fact, it prompted me to seek like information about my mother's family. Consequently, I interviewed one of my mother's older cousins who had records tracing my maternal grandfather's family back to the revolutionary war. I remember this particular grandfather telling me, when I was a child, how his father had homesteaded Iowa land. I only wish now that I had listened more closely.

Now that I am retired, I have the time to record and pass on the family stories that I was told. The formal records, studied by genealogists, do not include the folklore that gives a family its uniqueness. The stories, along with old letters and photographs, can help reveal the personality of a long dead ancestor; just possibly that personality might emerge generations later.

Understanding our uniqueness is difficult at best. Knowing as much as possible about our ancestors might help. Encourage your children and your grandchildren to interview their oldest relatives before the relatives die. Help them document births, marriages, and deaths. A living relative can save a person interested in genealogy a great deal of time. It helps to know where people were born, were married or were buried. It also helps to know who did what. Consequently, I wrote the following information for my grandchildren concerning our family's military service:

Dear Grandchild,

Your Great, Great, Great, Great, Great, Great Grandfathers, Edward Dawson and Reverend John Foster I served in the Revolutionary War.

Your Great, Great, Great Uncles, Peter Fuhs and Charles Wesley Moore served in the Civil War.

Your Great Grandfather Edward Fuhs served in World War I.

Your Great Uncle Ernest Fuhs served in World War II.

Your Great Uncle James Fuhs, and your Grandfather Francis Fuhs served in the Korean Conflict.

Your Great Uncle Marion Fuhs served in the Viet Nam Conflict.

And this is only a list of what your paternal grandfather's family did to establish and preserve this incredibly free country in which you live. Love, Grandpa

New technology has made such research much easier if you know where to start. Extensive records are available now if you have a computer and if you are on-line. Software is also available for organizing and storing such information. Storing and passing on family information to the next generation is a time-honored custom in many cultures. We are now in a position to do so more efficiently than ever before.

32
LEARNING
JANUARY, 2000

We associate learning so much with schools and youth that we forget that it is a life-long process. This process continues, of course, beyond retirement. There seems to be no end to what any person is capable of learning. However, in order to learn, a person must want to. He must also be able to concentrate on something outside of himself. Any teacher soon learns that if a student is personally miserable, due to hunger, pain, worry or something of the sort, he won't be able to learn. This is just as true of a seventy year-old man as it is of a seven year-old boy.

Learning takes effort. It is easy to become lazy as we get older, when less and less is demanded of us. It is also as easy to become mentally lazy as it is to become physically lazy. However the fact remains that both our body and our mind need regular exercise in order to retain their health. TV encourages us to be lazy because it demands so little of us. Reading on the other hand, requires us to develop our own mental images. A fine writer urges us to create vivid mental pictures, exercising our mind as a bicycle would exercise our body.

A walk through a botanical garden can be a rewarding learning experience if one makes a conscious attempt to identify the many plants. A stroll through a museum can be stimulating also if one takes the time and effort to ponder the historical significance of the many items on display. Whether or not an experience becomes mentally stimulating depends on our approach. Curiosity and the resulting motivation are the keys to learning.

If I am planting a new plant in my garden, I am motivated to learn as much about it as I can in order to insure its success. If I am playing a game of cards, I am motivated to concentrate in order to win. Very little real learning takes place without real motivation. Teachers develop many different techniques to spark the curiosity of their students and motivate them to learn. As retired persons we must plan activities that will pique our own curiosity and motivate us to continue learning.

At this time in which we live, if one becomes interested in any topic and wants more information about it, the sources are almost unlimited. Libraries are available to almost everyone, and they contain books on practically every subject. If you have access to a computer, and can go on-line, the quantity of information there is also exceptionally varied and expanding daily.

The computer and word processing have also provided us with new ways to store information thus creating our own private resources to which we can refer at will. However, the mere accumulation of facts is not considered real learning. Learning also involves the assimilation of facts so that their significance is understood sufficiently to make them useful in our daily lives.

Therefore, we must first stimulate our own curiosity. Then we need to search for information. Next, we need to use that information in our daily routine. Finally, as learning takes place, our mind expands due to the exercise it has experienced. The overall result is a healthy mind, and a more exciting retirement.

33
FRIENDS
FEBRUARY, 2000

One of the devastating parts of retirement is the loss of the daily contacts with the friends we enjoyed as part of our workplace. Most of our friends were associated with our job. Since friendships are nourished by regular contact, such friends are lost after retirement. Some companies have retiree organizations, but it isn't the same as daily contact.

Therefore, it's important for a man to develop new friendships after he retires. Few people are able to maintain a happy lifestyle without having at least a few close friends. Friends give us emotional support during bad times, and magnify the good times by sharing our joys.

Men seem to develop friendships more easily in an active situation. They would rather work with a person than just talk with them. They would rather play cards than drink coffee. They would rather write a letter than talk on the phone. With this in mind, it would appear that men should become involved in a group project if they are to meet new people in a situation that will lead to forming new friendships.

And once you have found someone whose company you enjoy, how do you maintain a friendship? Mostly, by being a friend yourself. As stated before, that means giving emotional support if your friend is having a bad time. It also means unselfishly sharing the joy of their good times.

A card of condolence if your friend loses a loved one, a get well card if they are sick, or a word of encouragement if they are down, takes very little effort and can mean a great deal to them.

You can share their joy with a congratulatory card at the birth of a grandchild or the marriage of a close relative. They will appreciate a newspaper clipping if they've received an honor of any kind. These kinds of responses show that you care.

By definition, a friend is one for whom you care. Their welfare is one of your priority concerns. Any way you can demonstrate this concern will help strengthen your relationship. Friendships are maintained by frequent contact. Even pen pals must write frequently if they are going to maintain their relationship. Many friends make daily contact, either in person or by phone.

The computer has made frequent contact even easier. E-mail is used frequently by my family, although I don't find it as satisfying as a voice or a letter.

A quote from Eugene Kennedy's book entitled, "The Joy of Being Human", states our relationship to our fellow man most succinctly: "Hope is the vision we possess of what we can be and what we can realistically build in the world, in which we understand that all we really have is each other."

34
SIMPLICITY
FEBRUARY, 2000

A lot has been written about simplifying one's lifestyle. However, no two people would agree on what simplification actually means. For one person it might mean walking instead of riding; for another it might mean a taxi instead of a limo. Whatever the approach, it should mean, for anyone involved, that they would like to experience less stress and more opportunities to relax and enjoy life.

For me, simplification means being aware of and consciously enjoying the simple things in life. I truly enjoy pulling on a quality pair of socks, appropriate to the occasion. I prefer a fine bowl of soup over any steak I've ever eaten. Walking, when practical, does add something very pleasurable for me to any journey. And a short nap, at the right time, can restore my comfort level immeasurably.

Simple things in life not only cost less, they help one develop a healthier perspective. Ornamentation on anything attracts attention, but does not necessarily produce a more useful or beautiful object. Clothes are an excellent example.

So how does one arrive at true simplicity? First we must carefully analyze our objective. If it's going somewhere, and biking is possible and practical, then biking might be simplicity. If it's a healthy diet, and cooking is possible and practical, then preparing one's own meals might be simplicity. If it's the need for exercise, and walking is possible and practical, then walking might be simplicity. If it's communicating, and writing a letter is possible and practical, then writing a letter might be simplicity.

Simplicity doesn't mean the fastest or the most technologically advanced way to accomplish a goal. It might very well mean the slowest and most primitive. When time is not a factor, such as in retirement, striving for simplicity can have many intangible benefits. The very act of slowing down allows us time to savor the experience. Such savoring enhances both our appreciation and our enjoyment.

Even in my study of flowers, I have found that if I am familiar with the simple wild flower from which the exotic hybrid is developed, then I have a better understanding and appreciation of the flower.

I realize that in our present society many people live complex, hectic lifestyles over which they seem to have little control. This is not true for a retired person. We have the time and opportunity to truly simplify our lives. However, modern technology tempts us to abandon simplicity. It takes less effort to ride than to walk. It takes less effort to watch television than to read a book. It takes less effort to e-mail than to write a letter. Simplicity is a complicated concept. I believe that no two people would agree on what it actually means.

35
HANDYMAN
FEBRUARY, 2000

In most every neighborhood there used to be a handyman. He was usually an older person with plenty of time. At least he never seemed to be in a hurry. In fact, if you wanted a rush-job, he probably wasn't interested. However, it was common knowledge that he could fix anything. I would guess that this gentleman was blessed with a great deal of mechanical aptitude. Even more important he appeared to be an accomplished problem-solver. As one used to say, "He had a lot of good common sense."

Handymen are hard to find these days. Part of the reason is city ordinances. Many cities require licensed repairmen and city permits for most repair jobs. We have printed numerous books for the do-it-yourselfers, but few working persons have the time to do their own home repair. They also frequently lack the necessary skills. Therefore we tend to hire someone to do the work. When hiring someone, we don't want to take any risks, and so we want the worker to be bonded as well as licensed. Such running scared and lack of trust makes the job of a handyman appear less and less attractive.

However, the main reason that we don't have handymen now-a-days is due to the fact that we show them so little respect. The man who fixes the toaster gets a lot less respect than the man with a computer who buys a new toaster on-line.

Working with one's hands no longer carries the prestige that it once did. Yet, we need fine carpenters, electricians, plumbers, painters, and masons more now than we ever have. An engineer is important to plan the job, but without the craftsmen the job will never be completed.

If a retired person enjoys physical work and has acquired the skills necessary to do the job, there are segments of our present society that would greatly appreciate his sharing his abilities. One growing segment is the elderly person who is no longer able to do their own maintenance work. Any older widow will tell you that contractors hesitate to bid on a small job. It is especially hard to find anyone who wants to do renovation work on an older home. If you are interested in doing this kind of work, it is usually sufficient to just let your neighborhood know that you have the time and inclination. Word-of-mouth advertising seems to do the rest.

I knew a man who ran a hardware store until he decided he could no longer compete with the chain stores. I met him one day after he had closed his store, and I asked him how he was doing. He told me he was doing odd jobs for the numerous widows in our old neighborhood. He also told me that he was making more money than he had ever made running the hardware store. He also seemed to be experiencing less stress, and appeared to be a much happier man. His story confirmed my suspicions that our society needs handymen maybe more today than it ever did.

36
MARRIAGE
MARCH, 2000

There are various times during a marriage when a change of some kind forces an adjustment in the marriage relationship. The birth of the first child is a classic example of such a change. A new job or a new location could also force major adjustments. Retirement is one of these changes. The marriage relationship has to adjust after retirement if the people involved are going to be happy.

Everyone has heard some wife complain, after her husband retires, that he is driving her crazy. Having him around twenty-four hours a day proves to be suffocating. He is constantly violating her space. In fact, that seems to be the problem: space.

Most people feel more comfortable if they have time and space that they can call their own. Granted, happily married couples frequently enjoy sharing time and space, but not for twenty-four hours a day, and not in each other's presence during all of that time.

First of all, it might help if each person has a room or at least an area that is primarily theirs. She has her sewing room or studio. He has his office or workshop. Each is a sort of retreat where they can spend time alone, amidst things and activities that they enjoy. Such a place has a special aura that reflects the personality of its owner and consequently one in which the owner is relaxed and comfortable. The emotional recharging that occurs in such an atmosphere is very important to one's mental and physical health.

There are also many activities available to retired couples outside the home. These present a different kind of problem. Ideally, couples can find such activities in which they are both interested and can share. However, over the years they have probably discovered that he enjoys activities that she does not, and that she enjoys activities from which he gets no pleasure. This does not mean that they are incompatible and do not love each other any longer. It only means that they are two separate people and always will be. No two individuals would share all likes and dislikes.

The solution for this problem requires each person involved to feel free to spend some of his or her time pursuing their own unique interests. Couples who have spent most of their lives sharing what little free time they had, can feel very uncomfortable going their own way even for a short period of time each day. However, one should not feel selfish, or guilty of neglecting their spouse, just because they are pursuing something that they truly enjoy. If it makes them a happier person, then they will be a better companion during the time they do spend with their spouse.

Since there is probably a limited amount of discretionary funds in your budget, then each person should get his or her own share to spend on their personal pursuits. No one person's interests can dominate the couple's time and resources if both of them are going to be happy.

It's also merely an act of courtesy to make sure your spouse knows where you are, and when you will return from whatever you are doing. This is one way of sharing, even though you are not physically together.

37
REGRESSION
OCTOBER, 2002

Regressive behavior is usually defined as behavior normally associated with an earlier stage of development. Many professionals say that this kind of behavior is caused by trauma and the resultant feeling of insecurity, which causes the person to regress to an earlier stage, where they feel more comfortable.

I disagree with this theory. I believe regression is actually the absence of behavior that is normally controlled by the subconscious. A common example is a child who has been toilet trained who no longer seems to be, after his parents get a divorce. A pregnant woman unintentionally dropping an article that she would normally hold, without thinking about it, would be another example. It could also be an angry driver failing to see a red light.

I believe that we associate such regressive behavior with trauma and the resultant mental anguish because, under those circumstances, our subconscious doesn't operate effectively. This explains why, under intense fear, an adult might urinate unintentionally. It would also explain why a toilet trained child might start bedwetting when his parents are going through a divorce.

As we mature, we learn a great deal of conditional behavior which is performed automatically. Speech is certainly an example. In fact, if a young child starts stuttering, and is then told to think about his speech, the stuttering will become worse.

Much of an emotionally healthy person's behavior requires no conscious thought. When such behavior becomes erratic, it is wise to examine carefully anything that might be causing undue stress.

What does this have to do with the older person? I believe the aging process also diminishes the efficiency of our subconscious. Why do older persons drive more slowly? They must concentrate on everything they do, whereas in younger persons, most driving behavior is performed without consciously thinking about it. Why do older people frequently fall? In addition to losing some of their coordination they also lose the automatic aspect normally associated with walking. Incontinence in older people is also due to a combination of physical weakness and loss of subconscious control.

A practical approach for most of us, in dealing with this phenomenon as we age, is to take sensible precautions. When driving, I concentrate only on my driving. When navigating steps, I always grasp the hand rail. I never miss a chance to use the restroom when we are traveling. Aging gracefully involves recognizing our limitations and behaving accordingly.

38
ONE UPPING
NOVEMBER, 2002

Everywhere I go my friends insist on discussing their latest medical accomplishments. I only find it irritating because I am a very competitive conversationalist, and I can never come up with anything as impressive as my friends.

Fourteen years ago, when I had my heart attack, I thought I finally had something that I could talk about. Unfortunately, all my cardiologist came up with was a simple angioplasty. Everyone I talked with had either had a multiple by-pass, a valve replacement, or a transplant.

A few years later, my family doctor didn't like the looks of my ugly moles, so he referred me to a dermatologist. The dermatologist said the moles were fine but he found a little carcinoma on my shoulder. Surely now I could discuss my skin cancer. The first person that I mentioned it to showed me her mutilated nose, and told me about her friend who had died of melanoma.

Moving on, so to speak... After a little blood in the feces, my family doctor referred me to a proctologist. Of course the proctologist insisted on a colonoscopy. After finding absolutely nothing of interest, he told me to stop taking the daily, coated aspirin that my cardiologist had prescribed nine years earlier. Furthermore, I discovered that all of my friends had had colonoscopies, but nobody wanted to talk about them.

More recently, my family doctor referred me to a urologist.

Although this long-fingered, friendly guy found nothing I needed to worry about, he still insisted on a yearly visit.

Very recently, I had a heel start hurting. I told a friend about it and she told me a horror story about having a bone spur removed by cutting the Achilles tendon and reattaching it. I went to Wal-Mart, bought a pair of Dr. Scholl's shoes, and ignored the pain until it went away. I didn't end up with anything to talk about, but at least I didn't get referred to another specialist.

I'm not going to get a flu shot this year. With any luck at all, I should be able to contract the flu. Then I can brag about being the only senior citizen in this city suffering flu symptoms.

They wonder why Medicare is going broke. Here I am, reasonably healthy, operating on a first-name basis with a cardiologist, a dermatologist, a proctologist, and a urologist, all of whom I must see on a yearly basis. My poor family doctor is thinking about retiring. He might as well. The only reason anyone goes to see him anymore is for friendly conversation and a referral.

I was thinking about all of this during Christmas vacation. When Mary found out that she was pregnant, what did she do? She didn't rush out and find an obstetrician. She went on a long, rough, road trip to see her cousin. Her cousin, by the way, was pregnant in her old age, and I don't recall anyone mentioning anything about an embryonic implant.

39
GRANDFATHERING
NOVEMBER, 2003

This grandfathering thing has its down side. Some interesting behavior is expected from the model grandfather. Since grandfathers have unlimited free time, they are expected to attend all kinds of events. Personally, I don't think any sane person should have to watch T-Ball. Furthermore, one doesn't have to be a Michael Jordan to realize that basketball wasn't designed for first or second graders.

I like to dance, but I find it painful to watch little people at a dance recital where more than half of them are not moving in time to the music. As for instrumental music, no beginning violinist should be allowed to perform in public during the first four years of their training.

Grandchildren also like to be entertained when they are visiting grandparents. No matter how many toys are available they want you to play with them. There are games especially designed for children too young to play games. Maybe it's me, but I just can't get really involved in Chutes & Ladders. And when they get old enough to play checkers, I'm supposed to let them win. Then if everything else fails, there are always the videos. I've watched "Bambi" so many times that I don't cry anymore when his mother gets shot. I could play any part in "An American Tail" and never miss a line.

Have you ever tried eating a meal with a grandchild? I've sat down to a Thanksgiving feast and watched a grandchild eat a lone peanut butter sandwich. You have to prepare twice as much Kool-

Aid as you would normally need because half of it will be spilled.

I would also like to mention the sex bias grandfathers are faced with. Grandmothers are trusted to babysit with a grandbaby. Not grandfathers. Grandmothers are allowed to discipline a grandchild. Not grandfathers. At a family get-together in the park, my three-year old grandson picked up a club and decided to hammer my shins. Because I told him rather vehemently how hard I would clobber him if he ever did it again, grandmother didn't speak to me for three days. Actually, grandmothers have an advantage. They make cookies. They have softer laps. They probably even smell better.

The best thing to do with grandchildren is to take them for a walk. They notice all kinds of things that we adults miss. We've watched ants for hours. If you take along a garbage sack, they love to pick up litter. I guess if I were going to be perfectly honest, I would have to admit that being a grandfather is a lot more fun than being a father. It's just that you run into too many situations over which you have no control. But then again, you don't have the worry of being responsible for what happens.

40
CORRECTNESS
DECEMBER, 2003

I've heard that writing down what bothers you is very therapeutic. So here goes. I used to be a reasonably good conversationalist. I would still like to be, but I can't seem to find anything to talk about that meets approval.

For instance, if I say that I am proud of the job that the servicemen are doing in Iraq, I am accused of being in favor of killing the poor Iraqis for their oil.

If I say that our priest is doing a fine job, I'm accused of tolerating pedophiles.

If I say that the school chorus did a great job on the Christmas carols, I'm accused of being against the separation of church and state.

If I say that the republicans should do something about gun control, I'm accused of wanting to take way the right to bear arms.

If I say that the democrats should do something about abortion, I'm accused of not wanting women to have freedom of choice.

If I point out to someone that, "The Cat in the Hat" is a vulgar movie, I'm accused of not believing in freedom of speech.

If I tell some young lady that I think she is quite attractive, she accuses me of sexual harassment.

And, whatever I do, I'm not allowed to say something that is politically incorrect. I was singing one of my favorite Stephen Foster songs the other day. It goes, "The sun shines bright on my Old

Kentucky Home, tis' summer, the darkies are gay." Good grief, didn't Stephen Foster have any sensitivity at all. He surely knew that he should have written, "The African Americans are happy." It wouldn't have rhymed, but at least it would have been politically correct.

Actually, the only time that I feel free to say whatever I feel like saying is when I am talking to my next door neighbor. He never criticizes me. Of course, it could be because he doesn't speak English.

We have become so obsessed with never offending anyone that it has become almost impossible to relax and say what we actually believe. Such an approach to self expression has resulted in placing us in the position of not knowing whether or not to ever take seriously what other people are saying.

I don't believe in purposely saying something that another person would find offensive. However, if we must first mentally analyze everything before we say it, then spontaneous conversation becomes virtually impossible. Children sometimes embarrass us with their honest opinions. I find their frankness to be a welcome contrast to most modern adult conversation.

41
DOWNSIZING
JANUARY, 2004

Some years are a bit more traumatic than others. 2004 was one such; traumatic, but very interesting. One of those years of major change, and change at our age seems to take a great deal of energy.

Our six-bedroom, beautiful old Victorian house was a wonderful place to raise our five children. However, it had now become a burden to maintain. No one was willing to let me climb that forty-foot ladder in order to clean out the gutters; especially in view of my heart trouble. And my wife was exhausted after preparing our thirty-member family meals on the major holidays. We decided that the logical alternative was to find a much smaller house and simplify our life style. After all, there were a number of much more interesting things to do with our time and energy than maintain an old house.

We considered an apartment, but we could find none with any adequate storage. Realizing that we had to abandon a number our things, we still wanted a reasonable amount of storage for those things we were not yet willing to give up. We finally found a small, two-bedroom house with a nice yard in a quiet part of town. Our next step was to figure out how we were going to physically make the move.

The first thing my wife did was to place thirty large items on e-mail to our five kids. They were instructed to take turns and choose six items each. It took them about two weeks to do so, and they seemed to have a good time. That was accomplished in early December. At Christmas they came with their U-Hauls and took their chosen items home with them. These items included those for which we would have neither use for, nor room for in our new home. For example, large pieces of furniture such as the piano and organ, and also such things as two large sets of china.

In the meantime, our daughter and her husband had decided that they wanted to buy the big house. They had wanted more room ever since the birth of their third child. Their decision made our move, physically and emotionally, much easier to handle.

By mid January, we were all ready to make the move. First, with my trusty pickup I took three loads to the landfill, two loads to recycling, and two loads to Goodwill. We also called the Salvation Army and they picked up one hundred fifty books. And yet, after moving, we ended up with a basement full of boxes. It was obvious that we needed to have a large yard sale.

Moving from three thousand square feet of space to seven hundred square feet has both advantages and disadvantages. What are some of the more interesting things we are doing now with all this extra time, energy, and money? Well, my wife swims twice a week, I play euchre twice a week, and we did have a nice time for six days walking the streets of Paris.

42
ACCIDENTS
MAY, 2006

Accidents don't just happen. Accidents result from our inadequately anticipating the possible consequences of our behavior. Furthermore, we older people tend to suffer more accidents than other age groups. Some of our accidents are the result of our deteriorating physical condition. We don't hear as well, or see as well, or respond as quickly as we once did. However, I believe many of our accidents could be prevented by a more cautious life style.

We should always wear a seat belt when riding in an automobile. When going up or down stairs, it makes sense to have a hand on a handrail. One older person told me that you knew when you were getting old if you sat down to put on your pants. Actually, sitting down in order to put on undershorts, shorts, or pants is a good way to keep from falling during the process. Ladders are notorious for causing serious accidents. We should probably avoid using ladders unless there is no alternative.

One of the advantages of being retired is that we never need to be in a hurry. Consequently, we have no real reason most of the time to ever exceed the speed limit. For most of us this will be a major driving adjustment. However, it could save us from ever paying an unnecessary fine, and keep us from having an accident. It is also a good practice to drive at all times with the car lights on. Coming to a complete stop at every stop sign could also help prevent a fine or accident.

85

Bathing is another situation where many accidents happen. If at all possible, we should avoid showering in a bathtub. Slipping while in the tub, or falling, while trying to get in or out of the tub, is usually the problem.

Sudden movements can cause considerable pain. Our body isn't as flexible as it once was. Collisions result from sudden movements that catch persons around us by surprise. When we adequately signal, and move slowly, our chances for an accident are diminished. This is as true on the sidewalk as it is on the highway.

Protective gear is always a good idea; wearing a helmet when biking is an example. Wearing gloves, depending on the activity, might also prevent an injury. Proper shoes can also prevent an accident as well as provide adequate support. As far as shoes are concerned, it is also a good idea if you have shoe laces, to tie them in a double knot. Untied shoe laces can trip a person.

If you live in an area where ice forms in the winter, keep a melting material on hand at all times. Falling is a major cause of accidents among the elderly, and nothing will cause a fall as unexpectedly as ice.

If you must move a large volume of material, divide the material into light loads. Lifting causes most back injuries. These injuries are not only very painful, they can be quite difficult to analyze and correct. Since, by definition, we have a great deal of time; it should make little difference to us if we have a large number of loads.

If you wear glasses, make cleaning them routinely a part of your day. Your glasses will last longer, and you will be more aware of the details in your environment.

Most of all, if you need help, ask for it. Most people are glad to help a fellow man. You will not only be helping yourself, you will be giving another person a feeling of usefulness.

43
CHANGE
SEPTEMBER, 2006

Retired persons who work at making their retirement productive tend to become more and more aware of their environment. Consequently they become concerned about the changes that they would like to see occur. It's easy to become discouraged when considering the number of changes one would like to see, and realizing you are only one person. Furthermore, you are a retired person who doesn't have the influence you might have had before retirement.

It's important to realize that one person can make a difference. For example, in local government there is usually sufficient staff to correct a problem. However, there is not sufficient staff to locate the problem. If you see something that needs attention, look up the telephone number of the department responsible and call them with an accurate description of the problem and its location. You might be amazed at how quickly the problem is taken care of.

I called the maintenance department of our park board and reported a very loose seat on a stool in a public restroom. It was fixed the next day. I also called the street department about a large hole under a railroad trestle that a rainstorm had washed out next to a sidewalk. People had been complaining about it for months. After I called, it was taken care of in a week. Pot holes, lawns that need mowing, piles of trash left by moving renters or anything else that detracts from the neighborhood's quality of life, should be reported.

If you are concerned about a business that is not maintaining its grounds or buildings, ask for their public service telephone number. Give them a call. They are always concerned about public opinion.

On the other hand, spend at least as much time looking for the bright spots. If you see that someone has done a good job, take the few seconds necessary to tell them. In a restaurant, a tip will not brighten a server's day nearly as much as a word of thanks and congratulations for a job well done. If you see that a business maintains its landscape and buildings well, drop in and tell them how much you appreciate their concern for the appearance of the neighborhood.

It's also important to realize just how important your example can be. When I retired, I started picking up litter from the very busy one-way street on which I live. It was not very long before my neighbors were joining my efforts, and it made a significant difference in a relatively short time.

If you want to make a difference, it's not enough to notice only what is wrong in your environment, you must also be aware of what is right, and take the time and effort to show your appreciation.

44
CLIMBING
DECEMBER, 2006

We all have figures of speech that irritate us. One that bothers me is the one we all hear about the time we turn forty. It's called, "Over the Hill."

First of all, if life is a hill and we are over that hill; that means at some point we must have reached the top. Actually, life is not a hill; it's an infinite mountain. That is what makes life so intriguing. There need never be an end to new experiences if we are willing to keep on climbing. So what is "Over the Hill?"

It just means that we have stopped, turned around, and we are walking back down the mountain. The trip back down the mountain is not very interesting. It takes less effort than climbing, but we have seen it all before, just from a different perspective. If we live long enough to reach the bottom where we originally started we experience what is charitably called senility. Sometimes we call it second childhood. This seems quite appropriate since we are back to where we started.

But a continual climb is tough, and I think occasionally we might need to stop and rest. We might even want to look back to try to determine if we have followed a reasonably sensible path. But it doesn't appear to be wise to yield to the temptation to give up, satisfied with the height we have attained, and start back down the mountain. Neither does it seem possible to attain a certain height, dig in, and stay there. We weaken; start to slip, and then we find it almost impossible to start climbing again.

It's interesting to watch how some people tire very early in life and decide it's not worth the climb. Others climb so vigorously early in life that they literally exhaust themselves. Still others climb their entire lives, gradually becoming better and better at compensating for the problems of aging, but never losing their enthusiasm for the climb.

45
DEMENTIA
MAY, 2012

Most of us either know or have close contact with one or more persons suffering from dementia. Unfortunately, many people have decided that persons who have started demonstrating signs of dementia are on their way out with little chance of experiencing any more happiness. Actually most persons in their seventies or eighties will experience some form of dementia. It is manifested differently in different people. It might be memory loss. It might be confusion when dealing with time or distance. It might be physical balance. It might be an inability to multitask. Dealing with their loss will require them to alter their lifestyle, but does not need to affect their ability to enjoy life.

Much of their ability to continue enjoying life will depend on how they are treated by the people around them. If you have frequent contact with one of us who are beginning to show signs of dementia, keep the following things in mind. They do not come naturally.

1. If you observe us doing something or saying something that doesn't make any sense in your opinion, don't say, "Why are you doing that?" or "Why do you believe that?" In fact, don't ever use the word "why" when conversing with us. It's very annoying to feel that we have to defend something we do or say, and it's usually very difficult for us to do so.

2. If you observe us fumbling physically, such as trying to open a plastic-encased item, don't insist on helping us do it. We take

that as an insult, implying that we are incapable of doing it ourselves. In fact, don't offer assistance that isn't requested no matter how long you have to wait for us to fumble our way through the task.

3.   If you are conversing with us and we use the wrong word, such as Ted instead of Tony, don't point out our mistake, which indicates that you knew what we intended to say. If you know what we intend to say, resist the urge to correct us. Besides, by the time you have corrected us we won't remember what we said anyway.

4.   If we indicate an interest in doing something that you consider trivial, please humor us. Something you consider trivial might be the highlight of our day.

5.   If you are planning a special family event, don't tell us that all we have to do is show up. We would greatly prefer to contribute to the event, if only in a small way.

6.   Don't rush us. We can't think fast, nor can we move fast. If you talk faster than we can process the words, you will get the erroneous impression that there is something wrong with our hearing. If you are walking with us, there could be a number of reasons why we might prefer to walk slowly.

7.   It's important to realize that what we believe to be true is the only thing that is true for us. Your presenting proof that we are wrong is a waste of your time, even if we are suffering from only mild dementia. Consequently, if you openly contradict us, we could become irrationally angry.

8.   However, please continue to communicate with us as frequently as you can no matter how frustrating you might find it. Such desire on your part to communicate with us tells us that you still love us even though you realize that we are no longer the person we use to be.

The problem we are facing doesn't seem to be a particularly new problem. SIRACH 3, 12-16, "My son, take care of your father when he is old; grieve him not as long as he lives. Even if his mind fail, be considerate with him; revile him not in the fullness of your strength."

46
CONCLUSION
MAY, 2012

Does retirement actually suck? No, retirement doesn't need to suck. Retirement is whatever a man makes of it, and in our present society the options are practically infinite. The problem is not with retirement as such. The problem is the attitude of our society toward retirement. There is no indication that this attitude is going to change in the near future. Therefore, the retiree must develop ways of coping with the attitude successfully.

Upon retirement many men experience three distinct, negative feelings: an identity crisis, a feeling of little worth, and social isolation. As a man develops his new lifestyle, he simultaneously develops a new identity. If his new lifestyle includes satisfying experiences, he will derive from it a new feeling of worth. The feeling of social isolation disappears as he develops new friendships as part of his new lifestyle.

Happy retirement takes a great deal of effort. However there has never before been a time when a man's effort could produce such gratifying results.

Made in the USA
Charleston, SC
20 February 2015